calm reflections

calm reflections

inspiring lessons for a stress-free life

edited by jo ryan

TANGENT PUBLICATIONS

Published in the United States in 2004
by Tangent Publications
an imprint of
Axis Publishing Limited
8c Accommodation Road
London NW11 8ED
www.axispublishing.co.uk

Creative Director: Siân Keogh
Editorial Director: Anne Yelland
Production Manager: Toby Reynolds

ISBN 1-904707-13-0

2 4 6 8 10 9 7 5 3 1

Printed and bound in China

about this book

Calm Reflections brings together an inspirational selection of powerful and life-affirming phrases that have in one way or another helped people to live less stressful lives, and combines them with evocative and gently amusing animal photographs that bring out the full humor and pathos of the human condition.

We all have too much to do and not enough time to do it in, and rush around getting ever more tired and stressed out. These inspiring examples of wit and wisdom, written by real people based on their true-life experiences, enable us to slow down, rethink our priorities, and rediscover our love of life. As two of the entries so aptly put it—enjoy the little things, and take life as it comes.

So take it easy, relax, and chill out!

about the author

Jo Ryan is an editor and author who has been involved in publishing books and magazines across a wide variety of subjects for many years. From the many hundreds of contributions that were sent to her, she has selected the ones that best sum up what a stress-free life is all about—making time for the things you enjoy and finding personal fulfillment.

Keep calm.

In any situation, I perform a lot better if I'm as calm as I can be. Panic stops me thinking straight.

Breathe.

When I'm getting stressed
about something, my breathing
gets shallow and makes me feel
worse. By telling myself to
breathe, I can focus clearly as
well as breathe properly.

It's all in how
you look at things.

Sunshine is delicious, rain is refreshing, wind braces up, snow is exhilarating; there is no such thing as bad weather, only different kinds of good weather.

Fear less, hope more;
whine less, breathe more;
talk less, say more;
hate less, love more;
and all good things
are yours.

It pays to be nice.

Being nice doesn't mean drawing
the short straw all the time. Good
actions come back to bless me.

You get the best
out of others when
you give the best
of yourself.

There is no conversation more boring than the one where everybody agrees.

When all men
think alike, no one
thinks very much.

He who angers you

conquers you.

He who establishes his argument by noise and command shows that his reason is weak.

I don't have to attend every argument I'm invited to.

Silence is one of the hardest arguments to refute.

The purpose
of life is a life
of purpose.

Work, play, play play, play, work, play, play play, play, work, play, play play, play, etc.

Remember what the money's for!

Don't let work
take over your life.

Find out what you
don't do well,
then don't do it.

Eighty percent
of success is
showing up.

Hard work spotlights the
character of people:
some turn up their sleeves,
some turn up their noses,
and some don't turn up at all.

A successful person
is one who can lay
a firm foundation
with the bricks
that others throw
at him.

The roots of true achievement lie in the will to become the best that you can become.

No one soars too
high if he soars
with his own wings.

He who knows himself
is enlightened.

Empty your mind and the right answer will come.

When I try too hard to think of an answer it will not come. I think the Buddhists do the same thing to achieve enlightenment—just focus on nothing.

When they discover the center
of the universe, a lot of people
will be disappointed
to discover they are not it.

Real knowledge is to know the extent of one's ignorance.

Imagination is more
important than knowledge.

Knowledge is limited.
Imagination encircles
the world.

To imagine is
everything;
to know is
nothing at all.

Reality can be
beaten with enough
imagination.

If you can imagine it,
you can achieve it.
If you can dream it,
you can become it.

Doubts are traitors and make us lose the good we might win by being afraid to try.

Don't expect things to go right the first time.

Even the best laid plans go awry.

Never be afraid to go for plan
"B"—or to reevaluate yourself.

Everybody makes mistakes.

Mistakes are proof that you're trying.

When I look back on some
of the things I missed,
I am immeasurably thankful.

Hard times are inevitable,
but misery is optional.

The problem is
not that there
are problems.

The problem is
thinking that
having problems
is a problem.

Challenges are what make life interesting; overcoming them is what makes life meaningful.

The best way to escape from
a problem is to solve it.

To the man who only has a hammer in the toolbox, every problem looks like a nail.

You can only choose from the options in front of you.

Never waste time on wishful
thinking or on unrealistic desires.

We can try to avoid
making choices
by doing nothing…

…but even that
is a decision.

Any change, even a change for the better, is always accompanied by setbacks.

There must be an easier way.

If you don't like
something, change it.

If you can't change
it, change your
attitude.

You must be the
change you
wish to see in
the world.

If we don't change,
we don't grow.

If we don't grow,
we aren't really
living.

Only the wisest and the stupidest never change.

Do it now—

tomorrow never comes.

Enjoy the process.

There are many things in life
where the doing, the process of
creating or developing something,
is actually more important and
more enjoyable than the end itself.

Your time is the greatest gift you can give someone.

Enjoy the little things.

If I hurry through life, I miss out
on some of the best bits.

What lies behind us and what lies before us are tiny matters compared to what lies within us.

Everything happens to everybody sooner or later if there is time enough.

Until you value yourself,
you won't value
your time.

Until you value your
time, you will not do
anything with it.

Focus on now.

If I start thinking too far ahead
then I forget to enjoy the now.

True wisdom is to live
in the present, plan for the
future, and profit from the past.

Don't cry because it's over; smile because it happened.

Things often happen when you least expect them.

Take life as it comes.